Vishnu Sudheer Menon

Introduction on Support Vector Regression

GRIN Publishing

Bibliographic information published by the German National Library:

The German National Library lists this publication in the National Bibliography; detailed bibliographic data are available on the Internet at http://dnb.dnb.de .

Imprint:

Print and binding: Books on Demand GmbH, Norderstedt Germany
ISBN: 978-3-656-93017-4

This book at GRIN:

http://www.grin.com/en/e-book/294791/introduction-on-support-vector-regression

GRIN - Your knowledge has value

Since its foundation in 1998, GRIN has specialized in publishing academic texts by students, college teachers and other academics as e-book and printed book. The website www.grin.com is an ideal platform for presenting term papers, final papers, scientific essays, dissertations and specialist books.

An Introduction on Support Vector Regression

Vishnu Sudheer Menon
Department of Electrical and Electronics Engineering,
Amrita School of Engineering,

India

March 26, 2015

Abstract

Through this paper I wish to to give an introduction about support vector regression and also its various modes of usage.We will be seeing how this support vector regression is formulated and how its varies alternatives are derived.

1 Introduction

Support Vector Regression is a method used in foreseeing various changes in trends such as the rise and fall of stocks in stock market[1][2][3],time series prediction[4][5] and so on.
Before moving into the core of the paper it is important to have a glance through few of the important fundamentals .
Primal Variable[6]$\rightarrow$ An expression consisting of objective function and its constraints.The optimization process is then required to minimize the expression with respect to its constraints.
Dual Variables[6]$\rightarrow$ The primal variables are converted to dual variables through the application of Lagrangian multipliers.So now the objective function is a dual optimization problem were the goal is to maximize it.
Why is there a need for conversion from primal variables to dual variables while solving these problems? This conversion is done because primal-dual is a method of solving dual optimization problems.
For the means of providing input data for the problem a time series is chosen.Time series can be considered as a sample of input and there corresponding target vectors as $+1$ or -1 .They are depicted as XϵR^d,the input vector ,and Yϵ R ,the target vectors.So time series can be represented as $(X, Y) = (X_t, Y_t), X_t \epsilon R^d, Y_t \epsilon R$

2 Support Vector Regression

After acquiring the desired set of samples, we need to derive a function for it,a line equation is used here as we plot the samples as points and this equation connects them.

$$f =< w, x > +b \tag{1}$$

2.1 The need of a flat function

The flatness of a function[7] is judged by how well we can fix a trade off between its complexity and its training mistakes.The complexity of the function means how the tube(the objective function) moves about to accommodate the training samples.So the main goal in getting an objective function is to accommodate as much as samples while the function is as flat as possible.
Now the width of the tube requires to be minimized to ensure good generalization and flatness.This is done by minimizing $\frac{1}{2}||w||^2$
This can be written as a convex optimization problem

$$\begin{aligned} \text{min} \quad & \frac{1}{2}||w||^2 + CR^{\varepsilon}_{emp} & (2) \\ \text{subject to} \quad & y- < w, x > -b \leq \varepsilon & (3) \\ & < w, x > +b - y \leq \varepsilon & (4) \end{aligned}$$

Here C is a constant determining the trade-off between complexity and flatness of the function

$$R^{\varepsilon}_{(emp)} = \frac{1}{l}\sum_{i=1}^{l}|y_i - f(x_i)| \tag{5}$$

This is the emperical loss function which is meant for better generalisation.

2.2 A Brief Introduction of Emperical Risk Minimisation

Now we have to choose the best possible function f(x) such that the loss L(y,f(x)) is kept at a minimum[8][9]. This loss is the difference in the response of y,the target vector,of respective x and the f(x) for that particular x. Consider the risk function

$$R(\lambda) = \int L(y, f(x))dP(x, y) \tag{6}$$

So we have to find a function which minimizes the risk in the unknown distribution P(x,y). A method of reducing this risk is by the application of Emperical Risk Minimisation Principle. The principle is that we replace the Risk function (above) with with the Emperical Risk.

$$R^{\varepsilon}_{(emp)} = \frac{1}{l}\sum_{i=1}^{l}|y_i - f(x_i)| \tag{7}$$

By principle over inputing enough samples for the function ,theR_{emp} is expected to converge to the minimum value of risk,so thereby reducing loss and increasing generalisation.

3 $\varepsilon-$Support Vector Regression($\varepsilon-$ SVR)

This is modified method of Support Vector Regression.The concept of $\varepsilon-$ SVR is that we characterize the function as a tube of width 'ε'[4][5] ,such that any error lying within the area would be ignored.Now if an error lies beyond the width ε,it is given a value of a new constant $\varepsilon^{(*)},^{(*)}$ indicating that it can lie above or below the tube,for ε^* being below the tube.So for these errors the flatness of the tube will be compromised and they would be included in the path of the tube. So in general ,this method ensures that for any error within ε,the tube doesn't change or will continue in its existing path and for errors outside ε,the tube will stray away from its existing path . Now the function for the $\varepsilon-$SVR is formulated below

$$\min \quad \frac{1}{2}|w|^2 + c\sum_{i=1}^{l}(\varepsilon^* + \varepsilon) \tag{8}$$

$$\text{subject to} \quad y- < w, x > -b \leq \varepsilon + \varepsilon \tag{9}$$

$$< w, x > +b - y \leq \varepsilon + \varepsilon^* \tag{10}$$

$$\varepsilon^*, \varepsilon \geq 0 \tag{11}$$

We now form the Lagrangian expression of the objective function in order to find the dual optimization problem we need to maximize

$$L = \frac{1}{2} + c\sum_{i=1}^{l}(\varepsilon^* + \varepsilon) + \sum_{i=1}^{l}(\eta_i\varepsilon + \eta_i^*\varepsilon^*) - \sum_{i=1}^{l}\alpha_i(\varepsilon + \varepsilon_i - y + < w, x > +b) - \sum_{i=1}^{l}\alpha^{*_i}(\varepsilon + \varepsilon^* + y- < w, x > -b) \tag{12}$$

Here $\eta^{(*)_i}$ and $\alpha^{(*)_i}$ are Lagrangian multipliers and holds the condition

$$\alpha_i^{(*)} \geq 0 \tag{13}$$

$$\eta_i^{(*)} \geq 0 \tag{14}$$

For optimal condition the derivatives of the primal variables are found

$$\frac{dL}{db} = \sum_{i=1}^{l}(\alpha_i^* - \alpha_i) = 0 \tag{15}$$

$$\frac{dL}{dw} = w - \sum_{i=1}^{l}(\alpha_i - \alpha_i^*) = 0 \tag{16}$$

$$\frac{dL}{d\varepsilon_i^{(*)}} = c - \alpha_i^{(*)} - \eta_i^{(*)} = 0 \tag{17}$$

Now after substituting it in Lagrange function we obtain the dual optimization problem

$$\text{maximize} \quad -\frac{1}{2}\sum_{i=1}^{l}(\alpha_j - \alpha_j^*(< x_j, x_i >)$$

$$-\varepsilon\sum_{i=1}^{l}(\alpha_i + \alpha_i^*) + \sum_{i=1}^{l} y(\alpha_i - \alpha_i^*) \tag{18}$$

$$\text{subject to} \quad \sum_{i=1}^{l}(\alpha_i^* - \alpha_i) = 0 \tag{19}$$

$$\alpha_i^*, \alpha_i \epsilon [0, C] \tag{20}$$

as we have eliminated $\eta^{(*)}$,so we get 19

Now

$$w = \sum_{i=1}^{l}(\alpha_i - \alpha_i^*)x_i \tag{21}$$

Now after substituting no in no

$$f(x) = \sum_{i=1}^{l}((\alpha_i - \alpha_i^*) < x_i, x > +b \tag{22}$$

This is called support vector expansion.Here w is represented in terms of x_i,so it is independent of the input vector space and dependent only on the sample space.Hence the complexity

3.1 To compute b

The method of finding a value of b involves using Kaush-Kaun-tucker[10] conditions.The KKT conditions state that at the point of solution the product of dual variables and constraints have to be equal to 0.

$$\alpha_i(\varepsilon + \varepsilon_i - y_i + < w, x_i > +b) = 0 \tag{23}$$

$$\alpha_i^*(\varepsilon + \varepsilon_i^* + y_i - < w, x_i > -b) = 0 \tag{24}$$

$$(C - \alpha_i)\varepsilon = 0 \tag{25}$$

$$(\alpha_i^* \varepsilon_i^*) = 0 \tag{26}$$

The observations we can make from this is

1)For samples with $\alpha_i^* = C$ only are outside the ε insensitive tube , as ,if $\alpha_i^* = C$,then no =0,while ε_i^* exists.

2)There doesnt exist a situation where $\alpha_i and \alpha_i^*$ are at the same time non-zero.

So to compute b we can use these observations
1) if $\alpha_i \epsilon (0, C)$ then $\varepsilon_i = 0$ and $\alpha_i^* = 0$
2) if $\alpha_i^* \epsilon (0, C)$ then $\varepsilon_i^* = 0$ and $\alpha_i = 0$

$$\begin{aligned} b &= y_i - < w, x_i > -\varepsilon \quad (27) \\ &\text{for} \quad \alpha_i \epsilon (0, C) \\ b &= y_i - < w, x_i > +\varepsilon \quad (28) \\ &\text{for} \quad \alpha_i^* \epsilon (0, C) \end{aligned}$$

Another observation that can be made here is that for $|f(x) - y_i| \geq \varepsilon$,the Lagrangian multipliers are non-zero ,or in other words all the samples within the ε-insensitive tube have $\alpha_i, \alpha_i^* as 0$. Support vectors can be used for non-linear function by moving the input sample to a feature space H and then applying SVR to these new samples.

$$w = \sum_{i=1}^{l} (\alpha_i - \alpha_i^*) \phi(x_i) \quad (29)$$

$$f(x) = \sum_{i=1}^{l} (\alpha_i - \alpha_i^*) k(x, x_i) + b \quad (30)$$

Now here the optimization problem finds the flatest function in feature space where

$$k(x, x_i) = \phi(x).\phi(x_i)$$

4 $\nu-$ Support Vector Regression

In this approach ε itself is a variable and in primal form it is multiplied with another variable ν ϵ(0,1)[11][12][13].So through ν we can adjust the width of the tube and increase it's accuracy
So the primal objective function is given by

$$\begin{aligned} \text{minimize} \quad & \frac{1}{2} w^T w + C(v\varepsilon + \frac{1}{l} \sum_{i=1}^{l} (\varepsilon_i + \varepsilon_i^*)) \quad (31) \\ \text{subject to} \quad & (w^T \phi(x_i) + b) - y_i \leq \varepsilon + \varepsilon_i \\ & y_i - (w^T \phi(x_i) + b) \leq \varepsilon + \varepsilon_i^* \quad (32) \\ & \varepsilon_i, \varepsilon_i^* \geq 0 \quad (33) \\ & \varepsilon > 0 \quad (34) \end{aligned}$$

Now we use the Lagrangian multipliers to get the dual optimization problem.So we get the Wolfe dual expression for v>0 and C>0

$$\text{maximize} \quad \sum_{i=1}^{l}(\alpha_i^* - \alpha_i)y_i - \frac{1}{2}\sum_{i=1}^{l}(\alpha_i^* - \alpha_i)(\alpha_j^* - \alpha_j)k(x_i, x_j) \tag{35}$$

$$\text{subject to} \quad \sum_{i=1}^{l}(\alpha_i - \alpha_i^*) = 0 \tag{36}$$

$$0 \leq \alpha^(*)_i \leq \frac{C}{l} \tag{37}$$

$$\sum_{i=1}^{l}(\alpha_i^* + \alpha_i) \leq C.v \tag{38}$$

An important expression we can get here is of w in terms of α and $\phi(x_i$

$$w = \sum_{i=1}^{l}(\alpha_i^* - \alpha_i)\phi(x_i) \tag{39}$$

So we get the regression estimate

$$f(x) = \sum_{i=1}^{l}(\alpha_i^* - \alpha_i)k(x_i, x) + b \tag{40}$$

The values of b andε can be got through KKT expansions where $\varepsilon_i^{(*)} = 0$ and $\alpha_i^* \epsilon (0, \frac{C}{l}$
Certain observations to be noted here is
1)If v$\geq$1 then $\varepsilon = 0$,as it dosent pay to increase ε
2)If v$\leq$ then $\varepsilon = 0$ is possible as the data can be noise free and can be perfectly interpolated by noise free model.

5 Conclusion

The idea behind this paper was to give an basic view about support vector regression,$\varepsilon-$Support Vector Regression and $\nu-$ Support Vector Regression.The idea behind how these expressions came into being was explained clearly in this paper.For the purpose of implementing these models, using LIBSVM through MATLAB is recommended.

References

[1] H. Yang, K. Huang, L. Chan, I. King, and M. R. Lyu, Outliers Treatment in Support Vector Regression for Financial Time Series Prediction, *Lecture Notes in Computer Science*, pp. 1260-1265, Jan. 2004.

[2] T. Van Gestel, J. A. K. Suykens, D.-E. Baestaens, A. Lambrechts, G. Lanckriet, B. Vandaele, B. De Moor, and J. Vandewalle, Financial time series prediction using least squares support vector machines within the evidence framework, *IEEE Transactions on Neural Networks*, vol. 12, no. 4, pp. 809-821, Jan. 2001.

[3] L. Wang and J. Zhu, Financial market forecasting using a two-step kernel learning method for the support vector regression, *Annals of Operations Research*, vol. 174, no. 1, pp. 103-120, Jan. 2008.

[4] H. Yang, K. Huang, I. King, and M. R. Lyu, 'Localized support vector regression for time series prediction',*Neurocomputing*, vol. 72, no. 10-12, pp. 2659-2669, Jan. 2009

[5] R. K. Mller, A. J. Smola, G. Rtsch, B. Schlkopf, J. Kohlmorgen, and V. Vapnik, Predicting time series with support vector machines, *Lecture Notes in Computer Science*, pp. 999-1004, Jan. 1997.

[6] O. Chapelle, Training a Support Vector Machine in the Primal, *Neural Computation*, vol. 19, no. 5, pp. 1155-1178, Jan. 2007.

[7] A. J. Smola and B. Schlkopf, A tutorial on support vector regression ,*Statistics and Computing*,vol. 14, no. 3, pp.199-222, Jan. 2004.

[8] E. E. Osuna, R. Freund, and F. Girosi,Support vector machines:Training and application, 1995.

[9] I. Steinwart, How to Compare Different Loss Functions and Their Risks, *Constructive Approximation*, vol. 26, no. 2, pp. 225-287, Jan. 2007.

[10] L. Gunter and J. Zhu,Computing the Solution Path for the Regularized Support Vector Regression *Ann Arbor*, vol. 1001,2005

[11] P.-H. Chen, C.-J. Lin, and B. Scholkopf, A tutorial on v-support vector machines, *Applied Stochastic Models in Business and Industry*, vol. 21, no. 2, pp. 111-136, Jan. 2005.

[12] B. Schlkopf, P. Bartlett, A. Smola, and R. Williamson, Shrinking the Tube: A New Support Vector Regression Algorithm, 1999.

[13] B. Schlkopf, P. Bartlett, A. Smola, and R. Williamson, Support Vector Regression with Automatic Accuracy Control, *Perspectives in Neural Computing*, pp. 111-116, Jan. 1998.

CPSIA information can be obtained
at www.ICGtesting.com
Printed in the USA
456964LV00011B/32
* 9 7 8 3 6 5 6 9 3 0 1 7 4 *